THE ALL SAINTS' DAY PARTY

Written by Jerry Windley-Daoust
Illustrated by Shaylynn Rackers

DEDICATION

To my family:
for your love, encouragement, and craziness. —S. R.

For my five saints-in-the-making:
Ben, Maria, Julia, Alex, and Matthew. —J. W. D.

Copy editing by Sibyl Niemann.

26 25 24 23 22   3 4 5 6 7 8 9

ISBN: 978-1-68192-518-9 (Inventory No. T2407)

RELIGION / Christianity / Catholic

LCCN: 2019939978

Our Sundav Visitor Publishing Division
Our Sunday Visitor, Inc.
200 Noll Plaza
Huntington, IN 46750
1-800-348-2440
www.osv.com

Other children's titles from Our Sunday Visitor:
Paddy and the Wolves: A Story of St. Patrick as a Boy
The Little Flower: A Parable of St. Thérèse of Lisieux
Flowers for Jesus: A Story of Thérèse of Lisieux as a Young Girl
Molly McBride and the Purple Habit
Molly McBride and the Plaid Jumper

The nights are colder, the trees have lost their colorful leaves, and the sun goes to bed right after supper.

That means it is almost All Saints' Day!

Maggie and Max can't wait for the All Saints' Day party. There will be pumpkins and dancing and games and treats… and everyone will come dressed as a saint!

"What is a saint?" Max asks his mom.

Mom explains that the saints were people whose hearts were filled to overflowing with God's love. By their actions and their words, the saints shared God's love with others.

"Each saint loved God in his or her own special way," Mom says. "Anyone can be a saint!"

Maggie and Max have a big, fat book full of pictures and stories about the saints. The children look at the book for a long time, but can't decide which saint to be for the party.

The next day, Sunday, everyone goes to the parish hall for coffee and donuts after Mass. Father Bill is there, too, along with his two funny kittens, Peanut and Butter.

"We don't know what saint to be for the All Saints' Day party," Max asks. "Which saint do you think is best?"

Father Bill rubs Peanut's belly. "Oh, I don't have a best saint," he says. "But I have always been quite fond of Saint Martin de Porres. He was a Dominican brother in Lima, Peru, who was so good at curing sick people and animals that everyone in the city would say, 'Go to Brother Porres' if they knew of a sick person or pet. He was like a people doctor and a pet doctor, all in one!

"But do you know what I like best about Martin de Porres? He made friends with everyone! Rich or poor, slave or Indian, Spanish or African—Martin welcomed everyone with love and compassion. He was even nice to the mice!"

"A saint should be friends with all people," Max agrees.

On Monday, Maggie and Max go to dance class. Miss Melody, the dance instructor, teaches the kids a Spanish dance. The children are excited to show everyone the dance at the All Saints' Day party!

After class, Maggie asks Miss Melody who she should be for the All Saints Day party.

"How about Saint Teresa of Ávila?" Miss Melody suggests. "She was a great master of prayer. Even today, people read what she wrote so they can learn how to pray."

"That doesn't sound very exciting for a party," Max says.

Miss Melody practices a pirouette. "Ah, but her prayer made Teresa very happy, full of joy and always ready to laugh! In fact, she once danced on a table with castanets!"

"A saint should pray to God," Maggie says,
"and share the joy of God with everyone."

On Tuesday, Max and Maggie visit their grandfather to help him build a stage for the Pageant of the Saints at the party.

"Grandpa, who do you think I should be for the All Saints Day party?" Max asks.

"I don't know who you should be, but maybe I should be Saint Joseph, All these carpenter's tools would make a great costume!" he laughs. "Do you know what I think was the most important thing Saint Joseph did? He got up and worked with his hands and his tools every day, just like your mom and dad do. But he did his work for Jesus, so that Jesus would have food and clothes and stuff for school. Ordinary work becomes holy work when we do it for Jesus!"

"A saint does good work for Jesus," Max says,
"even if it is ordinary, everyday work."

On Wednesday, Maggie and Max go to church with their family to help serve a delicious feast. Lots of people come from the parish, but there are new people, too. Some of them don't have any food to eat at home... and some don't even have a home.

Tonight, Max and Maggie meet a woman named Queenie. After a delicious meal of lasagna and hot, buttered rolls, the children invite her to the All Saints' Day Party on Saturday.

"That sounds like fun!" she says. She reaches into her sewing bag and pulls out a beautiful cloth. "I know just who I should be!"

"Who?" Maggie and Max ask together.

"I would be Saint Josephine Bakhita, who was kidnapped and sold into cruel slavery for twelve years. But you know what? Even when things were bad, she had hope. She lay in her bed at night, looking at the moon and the stars. And she decided that her only Master would be the one who made those beautiful lights. Why, she loved God even before anyone properly introduced her to him!"

"A saint trusts in God,
even in her darkest hour," Maggie says.

On Thursday, Max and Maggie come home from gymnastics to find their older brother, Matthew, setting up all sorts of games in front of the house.

"I'm in charge of games at the All Saints' Day party," Matthew said. "Mom wants me to find games that the saints would have played."

"Oh!" says Max. "Tell me some saints who played games! Maybe I can be one of them for the party!"

"There are lots," says Matthew, "Saint Gianna Molla loved mountain climbing, and Saint John Bosco did tightrope walking, acrobatics, and juggling—he was a one-boy circus!

"But my favorite saint who loved sports is Saint Dominic Savio. Even though he wasn't the strongest or fastest player, everyone looked up to him as a leader, because he always stood up for what was right. In fact, he even stopped a fight between two boys by telling them to hit him first!"

"A saint stands up
for what's right," Max says.

On Friday, when Max and Maggie come home from school, their Dad is baking something in the oven. It smells delicious!

"You have to wait until Sunday to try it," Dad says. "It's special bread for the All Saints' party,"

"I still can't decide which saint to be!" Maggie moans.

"Well, maybe you should be a princess," Dad says. "Or a queen! There are lots and lots of saints who were princesses and queens, but my favorite is Elizabeth, the princess of Hungary. When she married Louis, the ruler of Thuringia, she became a queen."

"Did she wear a fancy dress and crown?" asks Maggie.

"Well, she was given lots of fancy dresses and jewels and things, but she was always giving them away to needy people, so mostly she wore plain clothes. She gave away bread from the castle every day, too. In fact, some people in the royal court were afraid that she would give away everything in the castle. They told Louis to make her stop, but he just laughed and helped Elizabeth give away more!"

"Saints are like that," Dad says.
"They have generous hearts."

Soon it is Saturday—the day before the All Saints' Day party! In the morning, Grandma comes to drive Max and Maggie to the store to get supplies for their costumes.

"But we don't know which saint to be!" Max and Maggie exclaim.

Grandma laughs and pulls them close. "They're all good in their own way, aren't they? That's what makes them so interesting: no two are alike, because no two people are alike."

"Do you think we could be saints—I mean, real saints, in real life?" Maggie asks.

"Of course!" Grandma says. "Each of us is called to know and love God in his or her own way. You are the only person who can be the saint God is calling you to be."

"I wonder what kind of saint God is calling me to be?" Max says.

"Hey!" Maggie says, her eyes twinkling. "That gives me an idea for the All Saints' Day party! Maybe the best saint to be…"

"...is Saint Me!"

Saint Martin de Porres

Peru • 1579–1639

Feast Day: November 3

Patron of barbers, African-Americans

"Compassion, my dear Brothers, is preferable to cleanliness."

Saint Teresa of Ávila

Spain • 1515–1582

Feast Day: October 15

Patron of chess, sick people

"Love turns work into rest."

Saint Joseph

Israel • First century

Feast Day: March 19, May 1

Patron of fathers, workers

"When Joseph awoke, he did as the angel of the Lord had commanded him." (Matthew 1:24)

ST. BAKHITA

Saint Josephine Bakhita

Sudan and Italy • 1869–1947

Feast Day: February 8

Patron of Sudan, victims of human trafficking

"I am definitively loved and whatever happens to me, I am awaited by this Love. And so my life is good."

Saint Dominic Savio

Italy • 1842–1857

Feast Day: May 6

Patron of choirboys, juvenile delinquents

"Blessed be the name of Jesus."

ST. DOMINIC SAVIO

ST. ELIZABETH OF HUNGARY

Saint Elizabeth of Hungary

Slovakia and Germany • 1207–1231

Feast Day: November 17

Patron of bakers, brides, nurses

"Lord, never do I want to be apart from you."